Operation Speedy Express: The History and Legacy of One of the Vietnam War's Most Controversial Campaigns

By Charles River Editors

An aerial photo of Fire Support Base Danger during the operation

About Charles River Editors

Charles River Editors is a boutique digital publishing company, specializing in bringing history back to life with educational and engaging books on a wide range of topics. Keep up to date with our new and free offerings with this 5 second sign up on our weekly mailing list, and visit Our Kindle Author Page to see other recently published Kindle titles.

We make these books for you and always want to know our readers' opinions, so we encourage you to leave reviews and look forward to publishing new and exciting titles each week.

Introduction

A picture of Major General Julian J. Ewell (center), 1st Brigade commander Colonel John Geraci (left), and Colonel Ira A. Hunt Jr., the 9th Infantry Division chief of staff

The Vietnam War could have been called a comedy of errors if the consequences weren't so deadly and tragic. In 1951, while war was raging in Korea, the United States began signing defense pacts with nations in the Pacific, intending to create alliances that would contain the spread of

Communism. As the Korean War was winding down, America joined the Southeast Asia Treaty Organization, pledging to defend several nations in the region from Communist aggression. One of those nations was South Vietnam.

Before the Vietnam War, most Americans would have been hard pressed to locate Vietnam on a map. South Vietnamese President Diệm's regime was extremely unpopular, and war broke out between Communist North Vietnam and South Vietnam around the end of the 1950s. Kennedy's administration tried to prop up the South Vietnamese with training and assistance, but the South Vietnamese military was feeble. A month before his death, Kennedy signed a presidential directive withdrawing 1,000 American personnel, but shortly after Kennedy's assassination, new President Lyndon B. Johnson reversed course, instead opting to expand American assistance to South Vietnam.

The post-analysis of war is a complicated and process that benefits from hindsight, and the involvement of the United States in Vietnam over about a decade was no exception. Never formally declared as a "war," the Vietnam War was not fought in clean lines or with clear missions. Viewers of the evening news listening to the "box score" of killed and wounded each night had at best a hazy notion of what was happening a world away in Southeast Asia. If anything, their leaders were both attentive to reelection and on a certain level were themselves unsure of what was truly taking place. A military draft that sent over 50,000 American soldiers to their deaths was triggered by a resolution sought by President Lyndon B. Johnson in a decision to contain communism in a distant Asian land.

  Over the next few years, the American military commitment to South Vietnam grew dramatically, and the war effort became both deeper and more complex. The strategy included parallel efforts to strengthen the economic and political foundations of the South Vietnamese regime, to root out the Viet Cong (VC) guerrilla insurgency in the south, combat the more conventional North Vietnamese Army (NVA) near the Demilitarized Zone between north and south, and bomb military and industrial targets in North Vietnam itself. In public, American military officials and members of the Johnson administration stressed their tactical successes and offered rosy predictions.

The Tet Offensive made President Johnson non-credible and historically unpopular, and he did not run for reelection in 1968. By then, Vietnam had already fueled the hippie counterculture, and anti-war protests spread across the country. On campuses and in the streets, some protesters spread peace and love, but others rioted. In August 1968, riots broke out in the streets of Chicago, as the National Guard and police took on 10,000 anti-war rioters during the Democratic National Convention.

The Vietnam War remains one of the most controversial events in American history, and it bitterly divided the nation in 1968, but it could have been far worse. That's because, unbeknownst to most Americans that year, American forces had carried out the most notorious mass killing of the war that March. On March 16, perhaps as many as 500 Vietnamese villagers in the Son My village complex - men, women, and children - were killed by American soldiers in Task Force Barker. The worst of the violence, carried out by members of Charlie Company, 1st Battalion, 11th Infantry, occurred in a small village known locally as Xom Lang. On American maps, the location was marked as My Lai (4), and when news of the killings leaked into the American press over a year and a half later in November 1969, it was under that name that the incident became infamous as the "My Lai Massacre."

The My Lai Massacre was possibly the single worst atrocity committed by American forces during the long and sometimes brutal Vietnam War, and it has been called "the most shocking episode of the Vietnam War." It became a touchstone not only for the controversial conflict but for the manner in which the American government had covered up the truth, which many felt was emblematic of the government's behavior throughout much of the war itself. Moreover, it damaged the nation's credibility, as well as the military's; as Reinhold Neibuhr put it, "I think there is a good deal of evidence that we thought all along that we were a redeemer nation. There was a lot of illusion in our national history.

Now it is about to be shattered." By the end of the decade, Vietnam had left tens of thousands of Americans dead, spawned a counterculture with millions of protesters, and destroyed a presidency, and more was still yet to come. As David H. Hackworth put it, "Vietnam was an atrocity from the get-go... There were hundreds of My Lais. You got your card punched by the numbers of bodies you counted."

Operation Speedy Express was a highly controversial military operation carried out by the U.S. Army supported by the Army of South Vietnam (ARVN) as well as regional and popular forces during the Vietnam War. It lasted from December 1968 until May 1969 and took place in the Mekong Delta's Kien Hoa and Vinh Binh provinces. The operation was a part of U.S. Army "pacification" efforts toward the Viet Cong, as American forces sought to interdict Viet Cong supply and communication lines from Cambodia and deny them the use of operational bases. Formally, the operation involved 8,000 U.S. soldiers and resulted in 242 American lives lost compared to 10,899 Viet Cong and People's Army of Vietnam

(PAVN) killed, according to Department of Defense records. Operation Speedy Express was considered successful by U.S. standards, as determined by the primary metric of body counts. However, while the number of Vietnamese dead, including civilians, is unknown, it is assumed to surpass 5,000, and the high number of casualties was attributed to the indiscriminate use of firepower, which included air and artillery strikes in densely populated areas.

The controversy surrounding Operation Speedy Express led to an investigation by the U.S. Army and the House Armed Services Committee. The Army was ultimately cleared of wrongdoing, but resistance to U.S. involvement in Vietnam continued to grow, and in the nearly 60 years since, modern historians have tried to uncover more about the controversial Speedy Express and whether it represented a massive war crime. Thus, even though it remains less well known than My Lai, the operation's notoriety has started to grow in its own right recently.

Operation Speedy Express: The History and Legacy of One of the Vietnam War's Most Controversial Campaigns

About Charles River Editors

Introduction

  North and South

  The Mekong Delta

  The Philosophy Behind Operation Speedy Express

  Controversies and Allegations

  Online Resources

  Further Reading

North and South

Before August 1964, the United States had already been heavily invested in opposing Vietnamese communism for over a decade, and with the benefit of hindsight, the American war effort that metastasized there throughout the 1960s may seem like a grievous error and a needless waste of blood and treasure on an unwinnable and strategically insignificant civil conflict in a distant, culturally alien land. Indeed, it is still difficult for Americans today to comprehend how it was that their leaders determined such a course was in the national interest. Thus, it is essential at the outset to inquire how it was that a succession of elite American politicians, bureaucrats, and military officers managed, often despite their own inherent skepticism, to convince both themselves and the public that a communist Vietnam would constitute a grave threat to America's security.

Vietnam's first modern revolution came in the months of violence, famine, and chaos that succeeded World War II in Asia. Along with present-day Laos and Cambodia, the country had been a French colony since the late 19th century, but more recently, at the outset of World War II, the entire region had been occupied by the Japanese. Despite the pan-Asian anti-colonialism they publicly espoused, Japan did little to alter the basic structures of political and economic control the French had erected.

When Japan surrendered and relinquished all claim to its overseas empire, spontaneous uprisings occurred in Hanoi, Hue, and other Vietnamese cities. These were seized upon by the Vietnam Independence League (or *Vietminh*) and its iconic leader Ho Chi Minh, who declared an independent Democratic Republic of Vietnam (DRV) on September 2, 1945. France, which had reoccupied most of the country by early 1946, agreed in theory to grant the DRV limited autonomy. However, when the sharp limits of that autonomy became apparent, the Vietminh took up arms. By the end of 1946, in the first instance of what would become a longstanding pattern, the French managed to retain control of the cities while the rebels held sway in the countryside.

Ho Chi Minh

From the outset, Ho hoped to avoid conflict with the United States. He was a deeply committed communist and dedicated to class warfare and social revolution, but at the same time, he was also a steadfast Vietnamese nationalist who remained wary of becoming a puppet of the Soviet Union or the People's Republic of China. Indeed, Ho's very real popularity throughout the country rested to no small extent on his ability to tap into a centuries-old popular tradition of national resistance against powerful foreign hegemons, a tradition originally directed against imperial China. As such, he made early advances to Washington, even deliberately echoing the American Declaration of Independence in his own declaration of Vietnamese independence.

Under different circumstances, Americans might not have objected much to a communist but independent DRV. The Roosevelt and Truman administrations had trumpeted national independence in Asia and exhibited almost nothing but contempt for French colonial rule. However, as Cold War tensions rose, and as the Soviet Union and (after 1949) Communist China increased their material and rhetorical support for the Vietminh cause, such subtle gradations quickly faded. Considering the matter in May 1949, Secretary of State Dean Acheson asserted that the question of whether Ho was "as much nationalist as Commie is irrelevant. All Stalinists in colonial areas are nationalists . . . Once in power their objective necessarily becomes subordination [of the] state to Commie purpose." (Young, 20 – 23).

Acheson

Ironically, France and the United States were at odds over strategy with regards to the region. In 1950, President Harry Truman signed Memorandum 64 of the National Security Council, which declared that French Indochina (Vietnam, Cambodia, Laos) could not be allowed to be pulled into communist rule. Truman subsequently dispatched the U.S. Military Assistance Advisory Group to offer administrative assistance to the French Union forces, but France opposed the presence of an American force in Vietnam, and all but ignored their formulating strategy. The U.S. was barred from all training of the South Vietnamese, and Paris refused to keep them informed of current operations or future plans. By 1952, however, the French did allow the United States to shoulder one third of the war's financial burden.

The French position was severely weakened by the capture of its stronghold Dien Bien Phu in a 57-day battle from March 13-May 7, 1954. It was to be the most decisive battle of the First Indochina War, in which the French were trounced by General Vo Nguyen Giap. A full tenth of the entire French manpower in Vietnam was situated at Dien Bien Phu, where 11,721 were taken prisoner, and 4,436 of them were wounded. Ho Chi Minh was able to repeat the strategy in other locales where the French could find no answer to defending against him. It was an equal disaster for the United States, which by now was funding 80% of the war budget.

Through 1954, the Geneva Convention allowed 300 days of free movement in North and South Vietnam, after which the borders would be closed. The French Air Force evacuated 3,400 refugees per day from northern airfields and the French Navy did the same, but when numbers became unmanageable, France asked the U.S. for assistance. During this period, refugees swamped Hanoi and Haiphong, seeking evacuation to the south. On August 17, the first of many U.S. and French naval vessels, the USS *Menard*, departed Haiphong for South Vietnam with 1,294 refugees aboard.

Operation Passage to Freedom occupied a nine-month period during the U.S. alliance with Vietnamese politician Ngô Đình Diệm. During the Geneva Convention's duration of free movement, more than 100 U.S. Navy and military Sea Transportation Service Ships evacuated 311,000 refugees, 69,000 tons of cargo, and 8,000 vehicles from the north to the non-communist south. Included were many soldiers who went on to fight for the South Vietnamese military. In addition, 5,000 people, mostly Catholics, fled to the south in French, British, and Vietnamese vessels. The refugee account eventually totaled over a million.

Diệm

Elections were scheduled to reform the country under one unified government, however, but the communists of North Vietnam were expected to win it handily. This was an unacceptable outcome for the United States, attempting to contain communism at the height of the Cold War. Meanwhile, Ngô Đình Diệm had taken control over South Vietnam with American economic and military support, in large part because he refused to hold elections.

Born at the turn of the 20th century in Quang Bihn province of North Vietnam as a member of one of the nation's noble families, Diệm served as President of South Vietnam from 1955. However, he caused the United States many promotional difficulties, and Diệm was Catholic, an unacceptable reality for the overwhelmingly Buddhist majority in Vietnam.

When French advisors and military forces left South Vietnam in 1956, they left the U.S. as the only exterior force operating in the country and all French Navy patrol boats passed into South Vietnamese hands. After 100 years of colonial rule in the region, France all but bowed out of the conflict, officially transferring its power to the former Emperor of Vietnam, Bảo Đại.

Bảo Đại

When the French left and the responsibility for training and weaponry fell to the United States, it was a condition that the U.S. military believed would greatly improve the situation. However, the Army of the Republic of Vietnam (ARVN) proved "ill-adapted"[1] to meet the northern insurgency.

---

[1] Britannica.com, French Rule Ended, Vietnam Divided – www.britannica.com/event/vietnam-war/French-rule-ended-Vietnam-divided

Officers were described as "apathetic, incompetent or corrupt – and sometimes all three,"[2] and by 1959, U.S. Military Advisors were authorized to accompany Vietnamese units on operations.

In September of that year, the Seventh Fleet deployed in the South China Sea with the mission of deterring communist guerillas (Pathet Lao) from attacking the U.S. backed government of Laos. In the same year, however, the Viet Cong guerillas and the North Vietnamese military, the Viet Minh, launched a strong insurgency against Diệm's country, marking the beginning of the Second Indochina War. In the south, support eroded for Diệm's rule, in part because of his Catholicism and persecution of Buddhists, and also for his unpopular agricultural policies. As the early 1960s unfolded, a marked uptick of U.S. naval forces, including aircraft carriers, was seen in the region. The first deployment of U.S. Navy Seals occurred in 1962, suggesting that the naval presence off the Vietnamese coast was more than an intelligence-gathering operation.

---

[2] Britannica.com, French Rule Ended

Diệm's persecution against the Buddhists of his own country grew more heavy-handed, and the U.S. was forced to withdraw support when he had several people killed at a festival honoring Buddha's birthday, after which two monks and a nun immolated themselves publicly. A coup followed in 1963, during which Diệm was assassinated at the hands of several of his generals. Ironically, America's first Catholic president, John F. Kennedy, was assassinated only a few weeks later.

Following the downfall of Diệm, South Vietnam had no replacement with the necessary qualities of leadership or political experience. The purge of Diệm resulted in a brief period of leadership by the Military Revolutionary Council, but there was no central figure to lead it. The Council recommended negotiating an end to the war with the North Vietnamese and a free election, but this was anathema to the U.S..

To say that the U.S. supported General Nguyễn Khánh, who suddenly seized control of the south and pushed the council out of power on January 29, 1964, is an understatement. The U.S. all but overtly installed Kahn, after which the South Vietnamese military carried out a "swift purge" of the Council, arresting numerous individuals. The purge was clearly aimed at a national uprising of Buddhists against the government, and Americans in Saigon remained indoors for the duration.

Khánh's ascendancy rejuvenated President Lyndon B. Johnson's belief that South Vietnam might be saved, and that the only way to stem losses by the South Vietnamese army was to increase a U.S. military presence there. By this time, the U.S. was already involved in a heavy bombing campaign on the border of Vietnam and Laos to disrupt northern supply lines, and U.S. military personnel were already supporting raids against Viet Cong strongholds in rural areas. American military advisors numbered above 1,500, and they were considered necessary compensation for Chinese aid flowing into the north.

Khánh

Johnson

Naval and air support was also in place for intelligence gathering and reconnaissance. The USS *Kitty Hawk* was the first aircraft carrier sent into the Gulf of Tonkin in support for aerial reconnaissance operations flown over Laos. She was joined in the Gulf of Tonkin by two U.S. destroyers, the USS

Maddox and the USS *Turner Joy*, plus an additional carrier, the *Ticonderoga*. The carrier USS *Constellation* stayed to the south for the time being.

The USS *Turner Joy*

Added to the intelligence operations of these ships was a military support role. The destroyers oversaw a fleet of Norwegian-built fast patrol boats, covertly purchased and transferred to South Vietnam. As Johnson and Secretary of Defense Robert McNamara increased aid to South Vietnam, southern operatives took control of the Norwegian patrol boats for actions against coastal facilities, with the destroyers close by off the coast.

McNamara

These patrol boat raids, conducted by the Military Assistance Command Vietnam - Studies and Observations Group, were carried out in conjunction with the U.S. Navy's coastal activities, known as DESOTO (DeHaven Special Operations off TsingtaO) patrols. These coordinated operations involved ships equipped with "a mobile 'van' of signals intelligence equipment used for intelligence collection in hostile waters."[3] The first Desoto patrol had been carried out two years prior by the USS *Haven* off the coast of China. The first such patrol off the coast of Vietnam was performed in the same year by the USS *Agerholm*. They had been conducted successfully off the coast of North Korea and the Soviet Union as well.

SIGAD-USN-467N was the special designation of the mission aboard the USS *Maddox*, the ship primarily involved in the Gulf of Tonkin incident in August 1964. It was to be the 18th DESOTO patrol conducted in the Gulf over the past two years. As each mission was carried out, it was decommissioned, and each subsequent mission moved on to the next letter in the alphabet.

To this point, the U.S., a major player in the conflict, had remained largely in the background. However, in the pre-dawn hours of July 31, 1964, U.S. backed patrol boats shelled two North Vietnamese islands in the Gulf of Tonkin, after which the *Maddox* headed to the area. Surprisingly, it found itself facing three Soviet-built patrol boats. The *Maddox* fired three warning shots, but the

---

[3] Military.org, Desoto Patrol – www.military.wiki.org/wiki/DESOTO_patrol

North Vietnamese boats continued closing unperturbed, opening up with machine gun and torpedo fire.

Only days before, on the advice of General William Westmoreland, Commander of the U.S. Military Assistance Command, attacks were to shift from commando raids on land to shoreline bombardment using mortars and rockets. Whether the north captured this shift in its own intelligence-gathering operations is unclear. Opinion holds that the north, fully aware of the destroyers' work, attacked them directly after being unable to catch the fast-moving patrol boats.

Westmoreland

The Gulf of Tonkin became the focal point of the North Vietnamese's escalation against the increasingly bold American maneuvers. The Gulf of Tonkin is situated in the northwest arm of the China Sea and is surrounded by China to the north and east, Hainan Island to the east, and Vietnam to the

West. It is approximately 300 miles in length, 150 miles in width, and has a maximum depth of 230 feet. The main shipping route comes through the Gulf of Tonkin as it receives the Red River, passing via the Hainan Strait between China and Hainan Island. The main North Vietnamese ports included Ben Thuy and Haiphong, and the Gulf of Tonkin has been a site of oil exploration between many international companies through the years.

In 1964, the *USS Maddox* was an intelligence-gathering naval ship stationed off the coast of North Vietnam for the purpose of gathering information about the ongoing conflict between North Vietnam and South Vietnam. The borders between the two sides were in dispute, and the United States was less up to date on changes in these borders than the two belligerents. In the process, the *USS Maddox* accidentally crossed over into North Vietnamese shores, and when the ship was sighted by North Vietnamese naval units, they attacked the *Maddox* on August 2, 1964.

Though no Americans were hurt, naval crews were on heightened alert as the *Maddox* retreated to South

Vietnam, where it was met by the USS *Turner Joy*. Two days later, the *Maddox* and *Turner Joy*, both with crews already on edge as a result of the events of August 2, were certain they were being followed by hostile North Vietnamese boats, and both fired at targets popping up on their radar.

The fighting on August 2, can be verified through a variety of sources and an accounting of materials expended. However, the mystery of the Gulf of Tonkin begins with what the *Maddox's* Captain John J. Herrick believed was a second attack that spanned August 4 and into the following morning. He reported to officials that there was such an attack despite lack of visual confirmation. The *Ticonderoga* passed along the report of an August 4 attack, with some visual evidence gathered by sailors and officers.

After this second encounter, Johnson gave a speech over radio to the American people shortly before midnight on August 4th. He told of attacks on the high seas, suggesting the events occurred in international waters, and he vowed the nation would be prepared for its own defense and the defense of the South Vietnamese. On the strength of Herrick's report, on August 5, as part of the retaliatory action, Johnson ordered aerial attacks against the coastline's patrol bases and oil storage facilities. These represented the first purely American attacks against North Vietnam, named Operation Pierce Arrow. Lieutenant Everett Alvarez, an American pilot from the USS *Constellation*, was shot down and became the first American aviator to be captured. Fellow pilot Richard Sather received the unfortunate distinction of becoming the first American aviator to be killed in Vietnam.

Meanwhile, Johnson had the Gulf of Tonkin Resolution drafted, which gave the right of military preparedness to the President without Congressional approval. The resolution passed shortly thereafter, giving the President the authority to raise military units in Vietnam and engage in warfare as needed without any consent from Congress. Shortly thereafter, President Johnson approved air strikes against the North Vietnamese, and Congress approved military action with the Gulf of Tonkin Resolution.

It would be years before the government revealed that the second encounter was no encounter at all. The government never figured out what the *Maddox* and *Turner Joy* were firing at the night of August 4, but there was no indication that it involved the North Vietnamese. Once upon a time, Johnson had claimed, "We are not about to send American boys 9 or 10 thousand miles away from home to do what Asian boys ought to be doing for themselves." By the end of the year, however, over 16,000 Americans were stationed in South Vietnam, and over 55 years later, whether the country entered the war on a lie or merely based on poor intelligence and faulty decision-making remains murky. It is now commonly accepted that part of the attacks never occurred at all, even as sailors and high-ranking officers have ardently continued to offer arguments to the contrary.

The Gulf of Tonkin is obviously located several time zones ahead of Washington, so on the morning of August 4, news of the attack was reaching the U.S. At 9:12 a.m., McNamara called President Johnson and told him of the intel warning he had received. General Earle "Bus" Wheeler called

Admiral Edward Grimm to ask if he had received any messages. Wheeler then called General Keith McCutcheon and asked him the same question, to which the answer was that he had received nothing.

Of all the generals and admirals, it was Wheeler who insisted most ferociously that the destroyers "clobber"[4] the intruders, using heavy air support if necessary. At 9:52, McNamara, Deputy Secretary Cyrus Vance, General David Burchinal, and Admiral Lloyd Mustin of the Joint Chiefs met at the Pentagon as reports continued to come in at an increasing intensity. At that meeting, target folders were examined, including PT boat bases, airfields, industrial complexes, etc. Captain Eugene Miller, a mine expert with the U.S. Navy, was asked to join the meeting to discuss the possibility of mining the important ports of North Vietnam.

In the next NSA meeting with President Johnson, McNamara briefed those present, and Johnson agreed that a swift and strong retaliatory action must be taken. Meanwhile, with a vision of three to six patrol torpedoes engaging the *Maddox*, McNamara

---

[4] NSA/CSS

considered the rules of engagement to take destroyers into North Vietnamese territory. Among the reports still coming in, one reported that two more PT boats had been sunk, and the *Turner Joy* claimed that she was illuminated by searchlights and fired upon by automatic weapons. The 12-hour time difference between Washington and Vietnam added to the urgency of the response, and Johnson, stirred to a rate of urgency not befitting the situation, could not back away. Despite his own misgivings, he declared that the retaliation would go forward.

At 11:30 p.m. EST, Johnson took to the airwaves and informed the American public of the attacks upon the destroyers, and of his intention to retaliate. This was seen as a defining moment, as North Vietnamese and American forces were not known to have faced off directly before and the buffer of the South Vietnamese presence was removed for the first time. Johnson wrote to Congress on the same day. He assured them that the United States must take "all necessary action to protect our armed forces and to assist nations covered by the SEATO treaty."[5]

---

[5] Alpha History, The Gulf of Tonkin Incident – www.alphahistory.com/vietnam/gulf-of-Tonkin-incident/

In his speech to the country, Johnson proposed the Congressional adoption of a resolution which would enable him to operate in Vietnam independently of Congressional oversight. In his speech to Congress, he seized upon the worst scenarios being reported from the gulf, exclaiming that "aggression by terror against the peaceful villagers of South Vietnam has now been joined by open aggression on the high seas against the United States of America."[6]

The wave of patriotism that accompanied the administration's response to the *Maddox* and *Turner Joy* caused any objections to fall by the wayside, and Congressional debate, which would surely have been held before the incident, was muted. A resolution was voted on by Congress on August 7, 1964 and was passed unanimously by the House of Representatives. The Senate vote was nearly unanimous, with Senators Wayne Morse of Oregon and Ernest Greuning of Alaska in opposition. Morse agreed that an attack on American destroyers was "provoked"[7] by American aggression, and that the resolution was an elaboration of the infamous

---
[6] Alpha History
[7] Encyclopedia.com

"domino theory"[8] (the idea that if Vietnam fell, Laos, Thailand, Cambodia, and the Philippines would soon follow). He added that the document being put forth at the same time at which American ships were passing within three to five miles of the North Vietnamese coast was "naught but a resolution which embodied a predated declaration of war."[9] Gruening called Vietnam "a putrid mess,"[10] adding that "all Vietnam is not worth the life of a single American boy."[11] Both dissenting senators went down to defeat in the following election.

---

[8] Erich Martel
[9] Erich Martel
[10] Encyclopedia.com
[11] Encyclopedia.com

Morse

Gruening

Ultimately, the Gulf of Tonkin Resolution, otherwise known as the Asia Resolution 88-408, bypassed the need for the president to consult Congress for a declaration of war, a power exclusively reserved to Congress by the Constitution. The resolution accused naval units of North Vietnam, and by implication its government, of violating "principles of the United Nations Charter,"[12] and the parallel principles of international law. This evoked the issue of North Vietnamese sovereignty, as the attacks occurred on

---

[12] National Archives Catalog, Joint Resolution for the Maintenance of Peace and Security in Southeast Asia – www.catalog.archives.gov/id/2803448

the northern side of the line. Essentially, the resolution was asserting that the division of North and South Vietnam was a temporary solution of the Geneva Convention, and the U.S. involvement had been called upon to assist a faction of the South Vietnamese government.

Compared with their predecessors in World War II and Korea, the average American soldier in Vietnam was considerably younger and in many cases came from more marginal economic backgrounds. The average American soldier in World War II was 26, but in Vietnam, the average soldier was barely 19. In part, this was due to President Johnson's refusal to mobilize the national reserves; concerned that calling up the National Guard would spook the public and possibly antagonize the Russians or Chinese, Johnson relied on the draft to fill the ranks of the military.

In all, between 1964 and 1973, fully 2.2 million American men were drafted into the military, and an additional 8.7 million enlisted voluntarily, or at least semi-voluntarily. Knowing that draftees were more likely to be assigned to combat roles, many men who expected to be drafted took the initiative to enlist in the military before the Selective Service Board had a chance to call them up. This was a risky bet, perhaps, but not necessarily a crazy one, because enlistees were less than half as likely as draftees to be killed in Vietnam.

Moreover, given the numerous Selective Service deferments available for attending college, being married, holding a defense-related job, or serving in the National Guard, the burden of the draft fell overwhelmingly on the people from working class backgrounds. It also particularly affected African Americans.

The American military that these young draftees and enlistees joined had been forged in the crucible of World War II and were tempered by two decades of Cold War with the Soviet Union. In terms of its organization, equipment, training regimens, operational doctrines, and its very outlook, the American military was designed to fight a major conventional war against a similarly-constituted force, whether in Western Europe or among the plains of northeast Asia. As an organization, the military's collective memories were of just such engagements at places like Midway, Normandy, Iwo Jima, Incheon, and the Battle of the Bulge. These campaigns predominately involved battles of infantry against infantry, tanks against tanks, and jet fighters against jet fighters. As boys, many of the young men who fought in Vietnam had played as soldiers, re-enacting the heroic tales of their fathers and grandfathers. The author Philip Caputo, who arrived in Vietnam as a young Marine officer in 1965, recalled, "I saw myself charging up some distant beachhead, like John Wayne in *Sands of Iwo Jima*, and then coming home with medals on my chest."

  Expecting a simple conflict of good against evil and knowing little to nothing of the local culture, American soldiers in their late teens and early twenties arrived in Vietnam and found a world of peril, privation, and moral ambiguity. Despairing of and for young rookie soldiers like Caputo, Bruce Lawler, a CIA case officer in South Vietnam, virtually exploded with rage: "How in hell can you put people like that into a war? How can you inject these types of guys into a situation that requires a tremendous amount of sophistication? You can't. What happens is they start shooting at anything that moves because they don't know. They're scared. I mean, they're out there getting shot at, and Christ, there's somebody with eyes that are different from mine. And boom—it's gone."

Indeed, with a few notable exceptions, the American military experience in Vietnam consisted largely of small-scale encounters. Understanding full well that contesting a conventional battle with the better-armed Americans amounted to committing suicide, the Viet Cong waged an asymmetrical guerrilla-style campaign that capitalized on their superior knowledge of the terrain, their closer relations with local villagers, and their deeper commitment to the cause. Viet Cong guerrillas wore no uniforms, did not always bear their arms openly, did not observe traditional battle lines, and blended in with the villagers who supported them. During the war, an American soldier was as likely to be killed by a land mine, a booby trap, or a hidden sniper as by an enemy he could see.

To the Viet Cong themselves, such tactics were natural and justified in a "people's war": "The soldiers came from the people. They were the children of the villagers. The villagers loved them, protected them, fed them. They were the people's soldiers." To the Americans, however, the insurgents seemed sneaky and treacherous, readier to hide behind women and children than to stand and fight like men.

Of course, such guerrilla tactics served to blur the lines between combatant and civilian. As Specialist 4th Class Fred Widmer of Charlie Company explained, "The same village you had gone in to give them medical treatment . . . you could go through that village later and get shot at on your way out by a sniper. Go back in, you wouldn't find anybody. Nobody knew anything . . . You didn't trust them anymore."

Faced with such a determined opponent, skilled in asymmetrical warfare and enjoying considerable popular support, General Westmoreland chose to fight a war of attrition. While he did employ strategic hamlets, pacification programs, and other kinetic counterinsurgency operations, he largely relied on his massive advantage in firepower to overwhelm and grind down the Viet Cong and NVA in South Vietnam. The goal was simple: to reach a "crossover point" at which communist fighters were being killed more quickly than they could be replaced. American ground forces would lure the enemy into the open, where they would be destroyed by a combination of artillery and air strikes.

Naturally, if American soldiers on the ground often had trouble distinguishing combatants from civilians, B-52 bombers flying at up to 30,000 feet were wholly indiscriminate when targeting entire villages. By the end of 1966, American bombers and fighter-bombers in Vietnam dropped about 825 tons of explosive every day, more than all the bombs dropped on Europe during World War II. As Secretary of Defense Robert McNamara wrote to President Johnson in May of 1967, "The picture of the world's greatest superpower killing or seriously injuring 1,000 noncombatants a week, while trying to pound a tiny backward nation into submission on an issue whose merits are hotly disputed, is not a pretty one."

Even by the summer of 1965, some could sense that something in Vietnam was amiss, and the public began to notice the chasm between the "peace" candidate and the rapid troop and bombing escalation. Johnson's Gallup approval fell from 70% in early 1965 to 50% in June, and below 40 percent by 1967. An inter-party rift was noticed when Congressmen Gerald Ford and Melvin Laird asked for $2 billion dollars more for the military budget, as Johnson tried to balance the money flow to his enormous social programs and the war. John Stennis, Chairman of the Armed Services Preparedness Subcommittee, criticized him for financing the war on a peacetime budget.

The "guns-and-butter"[13] dilemma grew more tense when Johnson was forced to cut $6 billion from his domestic budget, and small rodent infestations bills in poverty areas were rejected by the House. The Harris surveys claimed that Johnson "too often raised false hopes that the war would be ended, and that he was not honest about sending troops to

---

[13] Mitchell Lerner, Vietnam and the 1964 Election: A Defense of Lyndon Johnson, *Presidential Studies Quarterly*, Vol. 25 No. 4, Perceptions of the Presidency (Fall, 1995)

Vietnam."[14]

By the end of 1967, with nearly half a million troops deployed, more than 19,000 deaths, and a war that cost $2 billion a month and seemed to grow bloodier by the day, the Johnson administration faced an increasingly impatient and skeptical nation. Early in 1968, a massively coordinated Viet Cong operation - the Tet Offensive - briefly paralyzed American and South Vietnamese forces across the country, threatening even the American embassy compound in Saigon.

By the time the siege of Khe Sanh was lifted in April 1968, the initial Tet Offensive had been repulsed throughout South Vietnam. Indeed, in many American accounts, the end of fighting at Khe Sanh is identified as the final action of the Tet Offensive. To the North Vietnamese, however, the "general offensive, general uprising" of Tet was a longer-term project that would continue at least through September. In the words of Tran Van Tra, while the initial offensive had failed to spark a widespread popular uprising or significantly weaken

---
[14] Mitchell Lerner

allied military capacity, it had nonetheless "sent shudders throughout the enemy's vital points, and destabilized its military, political, and economic foundations throughout South Vietnam," creating an opportunity for North Vietnam to "continue strong assaults and compensate for…earlier shortcomings in order to win even bigger victories." (Werner and Huynh, 48).

  Nonetheless, the troops who carried out the initial offensive suffered heavy casualties. This was particularly true of the local Viet Cong guerrillas, who had made up the bulk of the Communist forces in the south. These networks of disciplined and highly-motivated guerrilla cadres had survived for years in the face of the American and South Vietnamese militaries by keeping to the shadows and avoiding large-scale pitched battles. In that sense, the initial Tet attacks granted General Westmoreland and his officers exactly what they had long wished for: traditional pitched battles against the VC. The result had been as bloody as it was predictable, with an overwhelmingly lopsided body count and the decimation of Viet Cong networks throughout South Vietnam. A continued offensive would require massive reinforcements. Thus, through March and April, perhaps as many as 90,000 NVA reinforcements were sent down the Ho Chi Minh Trail to infiltrate the South.

May saw a punishing new wave of strikes across South Vietnam, known as the so-called "Mini-Tet" attacks. NVA troops struck Saigon on May 5, and heavy fighting raged there, off and on, through early June. Even after that, rocket and artillery barrages regularly targeted the capital for weeks. Casualties throughout "Mini-Tet" were heavy, and though it's often forgotten, American casualties were higher in May 1968 than in any other month of the war. Hundreds of civilians were killed in Saigon alone, and tens of thousands (perhaps as many as 200,000 across the country) were displaced from their homes.

With this, the smiling mask slipped even further, inflaming the burgeoning antiwar movement. Although American soldiers didn't lose a battle strategically during the campaign, the Tet Offensive made President Johnson non-credible and historically unpopular, to the extent that he did not run for reelection in 1968. By then, Vietnam had already fueled the hippie counterculture, and anti-war protests spread across the country. On campuses and in the streets, some protesters spread peace and love, but others rioted. In August 1968, riots broke out in the streets of Chicago, as the National Guard and police took on 10,000 anti-war rioters during the Democratic National Convention. By the end of the decade, Vietnam had left tens of thousands of Americans dead, spawned a counterculture with millions of protesters, and destroyed a presidency, and more was still yet to come.

It was against this backdrop that Operation Speedy Express took place.

The Mekong Delta

Pacification during the Vietnam War referred to using American and South Vietnamese programs to not only win the support of the people of South Vietnam but also to defeat the insurgency.[15] And so it was in the Mekong Delta, where interrelated programs comprised the effort to win the hearts and minds of the Vietnamese people: Civil Operations

---

[15] "Counterinsurgency in Vietnam: Lessons for Today." The Foreign Service Journal. April 2015.

and Revolutionary Development Support (CORDS) and the Phoenix Program. Under President Johnson, the Office of Civil Operations was established in November 1966 to coordinate all American-sponsored pacification programs, including those of the Department of State, the Agency for International Development, the military, and the CIA. The Office of Civil Operations was headed by Robert W. Komer ("Blowtorch Bob"), a CIA official and member of the National Security Council. The office "strengthened Komer's and Johnson's view that MAC/V [Military Assistance Command in Vietnam] leadership of the pacification program was essential."[16]

---

[16] Hunt. pp. 71-75.

Johnson and Komer

Komer's position was that three elements were necessary for pacification to be successful, with the first being security for rural residents, which meant separation from the insurgency. This would require the second element, which was to weaken the Viet Cong by destroying their infrastructure among the rural populations and to develop and implement programs to "win their hearts and minds," or at least to tolerate the South Vietnamese government and U.S. forces. Third, Komer insisted this strategy had to be implemented on a large scale because the Viet

Cong controlled large parts of the countryside.[17]

In May 1967, as Komer was appointed to head the newly established CORDS, the organization would be responsible for providing military and civil support of pacification efforts. Komer was appointed as one of General Westmorland's three deputy commanders holding the title of ambassador and the rank of a three-star general.[18]

Meanwhile, the CIA described Phoenix as "a set of programs designed to attack and destroy the political infrastructure of the Vietcong." It was established based on the notion that the North Vietnamese infiltration of South Vietnam had depended on local support from noncombatant civilian populations. The organization was generally referred to as VCI (Vietcong Infrastructure). The VCI was charged with recruiting, political indoctrination, psychological operations, intelligence gathering, and logistical support. It set up shadow governments in rural hamlets.[19]

---

[17] Dale Andrade, James H. Willbanks. "CORDS/Phoenix – Counterinsurgency Lessons from Vietnam for the Future." Military Review. March/April 2006. pp. 77-9.

[18] This was the first time that an American ambassador had served under military command and been given authority over military personnel and resources. Thomas W. Scoville. Reorganizing for Pacification Support. Archived 06-29-2019, Wayback Machine, Center of Military History, U.S. Army, 1982. pp. 60-65.

[19] Mark Moyar. Phoenix and the Birds of Prey: The CIA's Secret Campaign to Destroy the Viet Cong.

When a hamlet or village was identified for penetration, attempts were made to recruit the local leadership and the cadres threatened them with reprisals if they refused. Those who refused were assassinated, often along with their families.[20] Once the Viet Cong controlled an area, it was used to house and supply Viet Cong fighters, develop intelligence on U.S. and ARVN forces, levy taxes, and draft villagers into the Viet Cong.[21] This activity was particularly pronounced in the Mekong River Delta.

The Phoenix Program was a subset of CORDS beginning in 1967 and was sometimes controversial. It brought together existing programs with similar aims: to gather and develop intelligence on the infrastructure of the Viet Cong in South Vietnam and to "neutralize" it. Obviously, the concept behind the Phoenix Program was not new, as similar work had begun in 1964 with "Counter-Terror" teams in many provinces. They were renamed as the CIA allegedly feared that the term "terror" would raise questions.

United States Naval Institute Press. 2007.
[20] Andrade..
[21] Moyar.

The Phoenix Program's work was accomplished by many means, including infiltration, capture, torture, assassination, and terrorism. Numerous organizations participated in the program, including the CIA, MACV, the U.S. Navy Seals, U.S. Marines, U.S. and Australian special operations units, and the ARVN, but the Phoenix Program was carried out principally by provincial reconnaissance units. These were South Vietnamese paramilitary units led by the U.S. military and the CIA. These "hunter-killer" teams made use of the extensive intelligence databases to find suspected Viet Cong cadres. The Phoenix Program also was allowed to arrest suspected communists under special laws. Those who had been identified as associating with the Viet Cong fell within this category.[22]

Typically, individuals who surrendered or were otherwise captured were taken in for interrogation, where they were often tortured. Methods included "rape, gang rape, rape using eels, snakes or hard objects, rape followed by murder electric shock ('The Bell Telephone Hour') rendered by attaching

---

[22] Rosemary Giles, Guest Author. "The Controversial Phoenix Program Was Created to Obliterate the Viet Cong" War History Online May 17, 2023.

wires to the genitals or other sensitive parts of the body, like the tongue, the 'water treatment,' the 'airplane' in which the prisoners' arms were tied behind the back and the rope looped over a hook in the ceiling, suspending the prisoner in mid-air, after which he or she was beaten; beatings with rubber hoses and whips, the use of police dogs to maul prisoners."[23] The torture was usually carried out by the South Vietnamese, with the CIA and special forces playing a supervisory role.

The Phoenix Program lasted from 1967-1972, and during its five years of existence, the program "neutralized" over 81,000 suspected Viet Cong members or sympathizers, with over 26,000 killed.[24]

Whether the Phoenix Program was successful is subject to debate. Its success was measured by how many enemy combatants or collaborators had been brought in, regardless of whether they were killed or jailed, and regardless of the tactics used.[25] The Phoenix Program became the subject of a Congressional investigation in 1971 and was

---

[23] "Phoenix Program in the Vietnam War." Facts and Details. May 2014.
[24] Andrade.
[25] Giles.

officially disbanded in 1972.

Well before the Tet Offensive began in January 1968, the Mekong Delta became a priority for MACV. It was a strategically vital region as it housed a third of South Vietnam's population and produced three-quarters of its food. It was also close to the capital, Saigon. The defense of the area relied heavily on all branches of U.S. forces which, over time, played a crucial role in reclaiming a large portion of the area.

MACV determined that establishing South Vietnamese government control in the Mekong Delta was necessary to defeat the insurgency, so as early as December 1965, a U.S. Navy river patrol force consisting of 120 fast boats was created to support the Vietnamese Navy in patrols of the main rivers of the Delta. The riverine unit was called Task Force 116.

By the following year, the Viet Cong were launching over 1,000 small-scale attacks a month against population centers in the Delta, so a Mobile Riverine Force (MRF) was formed in early 1967 to counter this by targeting and destroying the VC's main forces operating there. The MRF was composed of a brigade (consisting of several battalions) from the U.S. 9th Infantry Division and a Navy component called Task Force 117, which had a total of 186 assault craft. All U.S. Army forces involved in riverine operations were placed under the command of the 9th Infantry Division.

On December 31, 1967, the Lunar New Year that signified the beginning of the Tet celebrations, the Viet Cong attacked major towns in the Mekong Delta, many of which were overrun. About half of the ARVN troops assigned to the Delta were on leave for the Tet holiday, so the responsibility for defending the region fell largely on the 9th Infantry and the naval forces. The ability to operate in shallow coastal areas (called brown-water warfare, or inshore warfare) was crucial during this offensive.

Riverine units had two main roles during the offensive: providing mobile firepower and transporting Army troops. In provincial capitals like Ben Tre and My Tho, where the Viet Cong were relentless in their attacks, the MRF helped to turn the tide of the battles, as the Viet Cong were forced to abandon their positions while taking significant losses. Casualties for the MRF and the ARVN were light in comparison. Similar successes were achieved in Vinh Long and other cities, resulting in the liberation of a large swath of the area.

The MRF also facilitated the transportation of troops, supplies, and medical aid. Patrol boats and aircraft from the various services also played significant roles. The ability of the riverine force to consolidate their gains by rapidly deploying substantial forces before the enemy was able to consolidate their gains was key to the success of the American troops during Tet.

The Delta was not a hospitable place for soldiers. As one writer put it, "Laced with a thousand miles of tidal rivers and canals, the Delta was a terrible place to fight – leeches, immersion foot, mud, swarms of malarial mosquitoes, and red ants whose bite was so painful, one soldier recalled, "you'd stand up in the middle of a firefight." There was the constant threat of ambushes too, hidden beneath the water as well as on land."[26]

The Philosophy Behind Operation Speedy Express

Operation Speedy Express was, in many respects, a continuation of the United States' overwhelming use of firepower and mobility against an enemy that depended on stealth and close-in tactics. By 1968, the troops enjoyed little support from home as the war was increasingly being demonstrated against, so while the Vietnamese were fighting for a cause, the Americans were fighting for an ideology whose grandeur was beginning to fade. Furthermore, the world had become increasingly aware that large numbers of civilians were dying in the conflict.

In the Mekong Delta, the 9th Infantry Division's operations during the first six months of 1969 did not follow the norm of engaging in smaller firefights as had been the case from 1965-1968, when large battles resulted in a war of attrition. Following the Tet Offensive, during which the Viet Cong suffered considerable losses, the character of the war changed. The VC broke regiments down into smaller units to avoid combat and maintain more

---

[26] Ward, Burns. p. 356.

flexibility while they rebuilt their forces. At the same time, the 9th's operations were not, in the view of many, consistent with a "pacification-oriented strategy."[27]

In January 1967, as American forces began to operate in the Mekong Delta, Ambassador Lodge's deputy, William Porter, had been cautious to allow U.S. troops and the devastating firepower that accompanied them to operate there. The Delta, despite its rivers, creeks, swamps, jungles, and agricultural lands, was densely populated. Nonetheless, the ARVN had not performed well there, and the 25th Division had obtained a successful pacification record in nearby provinces, so it was ultimately decided to send troops to the area.

That same year, the Mekong Delta Mobile Riverine Force, made up of two Navy squadrons, was formed. Part of the "Brown Water Navy," it was tasked both with denying the Viet Cong and PAVN access to the waterways of the Delta and transporting troops into combat in the way

---

[27] Guenter Levy. America in Vietnam. Oxford University Press, New York. 1978. p. 141.

helicopters did in the air.

1968 had been a difficult and bloody year for U.S. and South Vietnamese forces. Resistance to the war already had generated severe political implications in the U.S. and the peace talks in Paris had haltingly begun. It was important for U.S. policymakers that the South Vietnamese increasingly take the lead in fighting the insurgency and in controlling the countryside. The 9th Infantry was assigned the role of supporting pacification and Vietnamization efforts in the Mekong Delta.

The 9th Infantry Division had arrived in Vietnam in December 1966, and one of its brigades (consisting of several battalions) had been combined with two Navy River Assault squadrons to form the Mekong Delta Mobile Riverine Force. This permitted the infantry troops to be transported on Navy troop-carrier vessels. They were supported by "Monitors," which were armored vessels. This was a strong parallel to the Air Cavalry concept that was commonly employed in the war at this point, but instead of being transported and supported by helicopters, troops used vessels. It enabled them to operate in difficult terrain, which had few all-weather roads. The famous monsoon season brought tropical rains from May to October, and the area was replete with rivers, canals, and streams. For areas of high population density such as Long An province, the 9th had special rules of engagement, but the reality was that the problem of preventing noncombatant casualties was acute everywhere.[28]

  Thus, by late 1968, increasing efforts were made to reduce control of the Viet Cong and the PAVN in the Mekong Delta region by disrupting and destroying them. In December, under the command of Major General Julian J. Ewell, the 9th Infantry Division launched Operation Speedy Express, which was planned as an operation that would combine South Vietnamese and U.S. forces. The latter would, according to initial plans, provide air and artillery support and play an advisory role, but as it turned out, American forces would play a dominant role in the operation, and one officer was later quoted as saying, "It is difficult for U.S. troops to know whether they are seeing a VC or an innocent civilian." Indeed, throughout the first half of 1969,

---
[28] Lewy. pp. 141-142.

the 9th Infantry Division appeared almost entirely capable of making this distinction.[29]

Operation Speedy Express focused on three densely populated provinces of the upper Mekong Delta - Dinh Tuong, Kien Hoa, and Go Cong – and Ewell had a reputation for insisting on performance, which was measured by kill ratios. He was said to be obsessed with body count, and if only using that metric, the results of Speedy Express were very impressive. In the first six months of 1969, the division reported having killed 10,883 of the enemy, compared to only 267 Americans killed, a ratio exceeding 40:1. Most engagements were small-scale, and about half of the enemy kills were, according to reports, made by air cavalry units and helicopter gunships. 40% occurred in night operations.[30]

As Major General Julian Ewell assumed operational command of Operation Speedy Express in December 1968, he came to the position with a distinguished military background. A parachutist, he jumped into Normandy during the June 1944

---
[29] Lewy. p. 142.
[30] Ibid.

invasion, and he later jumped into Holland in Operation Market Garden. Ewell also was present at the defense of Bastogne during the Battle of the Bulge, for which he was decorated. He served with distinction in Korea. Now, in Vietnam, he commanded the 9th Infantry Division.

In June 1968, Abrams succeeded Westmorland as commander of U.S. Forces MACV. While Westmorland had favored winning the war by brute force, Abrams believed it was important to increase the emphasis on pacification efforts. Ewell and Abrams had fought together and were friends, but Ewell disagreed with Abrams regarding the way to win over the insurgents. In his after-action report, written in November 1969, Ewell wrote: "I guess I believe the hearts and minds approach can be overdone…In the Delta the only way to overcome VC control is by brute force applied against the VC."[31] He was overheard once calling out to a subordinate, "Jack up that body count or you're gone, Colonel." In the same vein, infantry unit commanders were told they would not be extracted from the field until they had produced an acceptable

---
[31] Ibid.

number of enemy kills.[32]

Through the end of 1968, Operation Speedy Express principally conducted reconnaissance missions, but from December 10-13, U.S. and South Vietnamese forces launched search and destroy missions in which ground and helicopter assaulted suspected enemy positions in Kien Hoa and Vinh Binh provinces. Their objective was to find and kill as many Viet Cong and PAVN as possible.

In January 1969, these operations continued, and U.S. Army units established firebases to provide artillery support.

The following month, the U.S. initiated river patrol boats to interdict waterborne enemy activities. The fighting was furious, and reported Viet Cong and PAVN casualties were high.

In March, the search and destroy operations continued and increased at pace as the U.S. and South Vietnamese focused on clearing the enemy from these two Delta provinces. Additional fire bases were established to support operations.

---

[32] Ibid.

In April, in addition to the ongoing missions, the U.S. Army established civic action programs to win over local support.

Operation Speedy Express officially ended on May 7, 1969, and by then, Viet Cong and PAVN forces had largely retreated from the area.

American troops had the advantage by day, but it was clear the enemy moved almost as they pleased by night, so to even the playing field, the Night Hunter program launched by Ewell consisted of Huey troop transport helicopters that coordinated efforts with Cobra gunships. "People sniffers," instruments that could detect carbon and ammonia traces that could indicate people were below them, were installed on the bottoms of the helicopters.

OH-6A Cayuse helicopters were referred to as "loaches," and they flew low and drew fire to set up the shots for the Cobras circling above. When the AH-1G Cobra arrived in Vietnam in August 1967, it was fast and deadly. From the rear cockpit, the pilot fired rockets from launchers fixed to the stub wings on either side; the copilot in the front operated a chin turret that held a minigun and grenade launcher.

Loaches were paired with Cobra gunships. Loaches, usually with a pilot, observer, and sometimes a door gunner aboard, flew as little as 10 feet above the treetops and between about 45 and 60 miles per hour, scouting for signs of the enemy. Snipers were in the back of the choppers with night scopes. When anybody was spotted, the snipers fired with tracer bullets. This directed the Cobras where to aim their fire.

An AH-1 Cobra

Cobras, nicknamed Snakes, flew circles 1,500 feet above the scouts, waiting to pounce on whatever the Loach found. Once they found their prey, the Loaches quickly left as the Cobras rolled in.

Hugh Mills, who flew both Loaches and Cobras in Vietnam from 1968-1972, explained, "Most of our engagements were 25 to 50 feet when we opened up on them…I've seen them, whites of the eyes, and they've seen me, whites of the eyes…I have come home with blood on my windshield. A little gory but that's how close we were."[33]

People in black pajamas, frightened, typically ran, and were targeted and shot. Ewell's Chief of Staff, Colonel Ira Hunt, is reported to have told a major that they shot people in black pajamas because they were VC. When challenged by a major, who said that workers in their fields wore black pajamas, Hunt retorted, "No, not around here. Black pajamas are Viet Cong."[34] People seen running were considered targets, and there is no indication they were advised that they should stay still to remain safe.

Of course, it's crucial to keep in mind that the people participating in Operation Speedy Express were not doing so in a contextless vacuum. Much

---

[33] Donald Porter "Cobras and Loaches, two vastly different aircraft, relied on each other to fight the enemy. In Vietnam, These Helicopter Scouts Saw Combat Up Close." Air & Space Magazine. September 2017.

[34] Ward, Burns. p. 357.

has been written about the killing of civilians by U.S. troops in Vietnam, but far less is generally known about the extent to which the VC and the PAVN made use of terror tactics. Official estimates suggest that up to 227,000 South Vietnamese civilians were killed between 1954 and 1975, and murder, kidnapping, and torture were used extensively by the Viet Cong and the North Vietnamese during the war. These actions were principally directed at Vietnamese civilians with the objective of eliminating opponents, eroding the morale of the populace, increasing revenues from taxes, and, of course, for propaganda purposes. Methods of terror included murder and kidnapping, but also the mortaring of refugee camps, placing mines on highways used by the general population, and the shelling of cities with rockets. Americans read little about this, but American soldiers were certainly aware of it, as authors Michael Lanning and Dan Cragg noted, "This extensive use of terror received comparatively little attention from Western journalists, who were preoccupied with covering the conventional warfare aspect of the conflict."[35]

---

[35] Michael Lanning, Dan Cragg. Inside the VC and the NVA. Ballantine Books. 1993. p. 186.

The historian Douglas Pike made this argument in his studies of the Viet Cong, which were grounded in more than a decade living in South Vietnam as an employee of the United States Information Agency. Pike documented Viet Cong uses of terrorism, including the massacre of several thousand civilians at Hue during the Tet Offensive: "The seeming randomness of a car bomb here and an explosion in a market belied the calculated, rational nature of the Viet Cong's terrorism as a primary tactic in its war strategy."[36]

Tools of terror were used to communicate that the South Vietnamese government could not protect the population in their hamlets and villages. The insurgents killed men, women, and children to sow fear and panic.[37] Assassinations and other methods were first conducted by "Special Activity Cells," but later in the war such operations became centralized in the Viet Cong Security Service.[38]

The Viet Cong mainly targeted hamlets it thought supported the national government. The objective of

---

[36] Heather Stur. "The Viet Cong Committed Atrocities Too." The New York Times. December 19, 2017.
[37] Gunther Lewy. America in Vietnam. Oxford University Press. 1978.
[38] Edward Doyle, Samuel Lipsman, Terrence Maitland. The Vietnam Experience. Boston Publishing Company, 1978.

an attack followed the terrorist prototype: generally, to spread confusion and fear rather than to kill many civilians. In the rural countryside, guerrillas targeted hamlet chiefs, employees of the government, teachers, and suspected "informants" and other "traitors." These included foreigners such as priests and missionaries, humanitarian aid workers, and of course, American government employees.[39]

In 1967, the South Vietnamese State Health Secretary reported to the World Health Organization in Geneva that more than 200 doctors and health workers had been killed over the last decade and that 211 members of his staff had been either killed or kidnapped. Additionally, "174 dispensaries, maternity homes and hospitals destroyed; and 40 ambulances mined or machine-gunned."[40] Statistics show that from 1968-1970, 80% of the casualties were civilians, and only about 20% were government officials, policemen, members of the self-defense forces, or pacification cadres.[41]

Official Viet Cong documents reveal that the use of

---

[39] Stur.
[40] Douglas Pike. The Vietcong Strategy of Terror. PDF. U.S. Mission, Saigon. February 1970.
[41] Lewy.

terror tactics was encouraged. A 1965 memorandum from the North Vietnamese political and military headquarters in South Vietnam directed the Party Committee in Saigon "to exploit every opportunity to kill enemy leaders and vicious thugs, to intensify our political attacks aimed at spreading fear and confusion among the enemy's ranks." A resolution from that office published in 1969 said, "Integral to the political struggle would be the liberal use of terrorism to weaken and destroy the local government, strengthen the party apparatus, proselyte among the populace, erode the control and influence of the Government of Vietnam, and weaken the" South Vietnam Air Force.[42]

  The Viet Cong, supported by the PAVN, committed acts of terror on their own people as they were fighting a war against American forces. At times, they used similar methods and tactics. While the PAVN were regulars and tended to fight as armies, the VC were largely irregulars who fought a guerilla war.

  The Viet Cong walked a delicate line between

---
[42] Lanning, Cragg. p. 5.

instilling terror and fear, and provoking hatred for their cause. Thus, they endeavored to make it appear that the activities related to terror were unrelated to their political agenda.

All the while, rural citizens were caught in the middle. Heather Stur, in an article for the *New York Times*, noted, "Vietnamese civilians were under attack from all sides. The Saigon regime and its American allies came at them from one direction; from another, Hanoi and the Viet Cong with Chinese and Russian assistance."[43]

For American soldiers, the enemy was the perpetrator of evil acts of terror on a largely innocent population, as well as on their own fellow soldiers. They often saw mutilated bodies and evidence of unspeakable acts of violence. At the same time, they were at war with those perpetrators, who they insisted wore black "pajamas," which was the way many villagers dressed. In the minds of young soldiers, it became difficult if not impossible to distinguish who was the enemy, particularly as it was known that there were VC sympathizers among

---

[43] Stur.

the rural population. And some simply didn't care. These soldiers had been dropped into a country vastly different from their own, with people who looked and acted very differently from their families, friends, and communities. It was therefore easy to "dehumanize" the Vietnamese, making the commission of acts of terrible violence against them easier psychologically. This was particularly true when they were motivated to do so by their own leadership.

Ewell earned the nickname "Butcher of the Delta" resulting from his sanguine approach, and he was proud of the 9th Infantry's performance statistically, but not all members of the 9th Infantry agreed. One officer, Robert Gard, told Ward and Burns, "The idea that we killed only enemy combatants is about as gross an exaggeration as I could imagine…To talk about ratios of forty-five to one simply defies my imagination."[44]

At the same time, there was real concern that the reliance on a body count metric induced subordinates to inflate the number of enemy dead by

---

[44] Ward, Burns. p. 360.

counting civilians as enemy combatants, and by committing atrocities. This was almost certainly the case during Operation Speedy Express. In 1972, the Army inspector general estimated that between 5,000 and 7,000 of the almost 11,000 killed by the 9th during the operation had been civilians. There was also the question of captured weapons, because during the entire operation, Ewell's men captured only 60 crew-served weapons and 688 individual weapons from the large number of supposed enemy fighters. Ewell claimed this number was low because many of the deaths occurred at night, and because "many of the guerilla units were not armed."[45]

Nonetheless, in the immediate wake of the operation, the 9th Infantry's performance was recognized by senior commanders, and General Ewell was awarded his third star and given command of II Field Force, the largest in Vietnam.[46] That occurred even as the VC called the fighting in the Mekong Delta in early 1969 a strategic victory, claiming that their fighters and bases were left

---
[45] Ibid.
[46] Ibid.

mostly intact and their presence in the region was not removed by the operation.[47]

Controversies and Allegations

New York Times journalist Seymour Hersh was the first to raise allegations that U.S. forces committed war crimes and atrocities during Operation Speedy Express and killed innocent civilians, sparking a controversy that resulted in an investigation of the operation by the House Armed Services Committee. While the committee eventually cleared the Army of wrongdoing, the operation almost immediately contributed to the growing opposition to the war in the U.S. and elsewhere.

In the aftermath of Operation Speedy Express, there were conflicting accounts and assessments of its outcomes and the impact on civilian populations. Some military officials, including General Ewell, who led the 9th Infantry Division, defended the conduct of the operation and refuted claims of excessive civilian casualties. Ewell told his boss, General Abrams, that it was "the biggest collection of malicious innuendo I have ever seen,"[48] insisting

---

[47] Ward, Burns.

that the operation targeted Viet Cong forces and infrastructure and employed appropriate measures to minimize civilian harm.

Conversely, critics, including journalists and veterans, raised serious concerns about the conduct of the operation and its impact on civilians. Some alleged that the operation involved indiscriminate use of firepower, free-fire zones where any person could be targeted, and pressure on troops to achieve high body counts, leading to the deaths of civilians. Reports and testimonies suggested that innocent Vietnamese civilians were caught in the crossfire or intentionally targeted.

Journalist Kevin Buckley's article, "Pacification's Deadly Price," published in *Newsweek* in June 1972, questioned the high ratio of enemy casualties to U.S. casualties and raised concerns about civilians. He cited interviews and evidence indicating that a very large number of the dead were innocent civilians. This article and subsequent investigations fueled public awareness and debate about the conduct of U.S. forces in Vietnam in general.[49]

---
[48] Hammond. p. 239.
[49] Kevin Buckley. "Pacification's Deadly Price". Newsweek. 19 June 1972. pp. 42–3

Historian Nick Turse's *Kill Anything That Moves*, published in 2013, extensively examined Operation Speedy Express and argued that it resulted in many civilian casualties due to a combination of aggressive tactics, free-fire zones, and pressure for high body counts.[50]

The controversy surrounding Operation Speedy Express and the broader issue of civilian casualties during the Vietnam War contributed to public and political discourse about the conduct and justification of the war. It raised questions about the adherence to rules of engagement, the protection of civilian populations, and the impact of U.S. military operations on Vietnamese communities.

Since ancient times, the morality of warfare has been a subject of intense debate. The "Just War Theory," a doctrine of military ethics, has served as a framework for assessing the moral justifiability of war.[51] Divided into *jus ad bellum* (morality of going to war) and *jus in bello* (morality during the war), this theory has been scrutinized by policymakers,

---

[50] Nick Turse. Kill Anything That Moves: The Real American War in Vietnam. Metropolitan Books. 2013 p. 209.
[51] Marcus Tullius Cicero; Walter Miller. De Officiis. With an English translation by Walter Miller. Robarts – University of Toronto. 1913

theologians, and ethicists to determine the ethical criteria for armed conflict.[52]

Once a war is underway, the principles of *jus in bello* come into play, guiding the conduct of combatants. The first principle, Distinction, stipulated that acts of war should only target enemy combatants, sparing non-combatants who find themselves embroiled in the conflict due to circumstances beyond their control. Prohibited acts include bombing civilian residential areas that lack legitimate military targets, committing acts of terrorism or reprisals against civilians and prisoners of war, and attacking neutral targets or surrendering combatants who pose no immediate lethal threat.

Proportionality, the second principle, demands that combatants ensure the harm inflicted upon civilians or their property is not excessive compared to the military advantage gained from attacking a legitimate military target. Military Necessity, another principle, prohibits attacks or actions that do not align with a legitimate military objective, aiming to curtail excessive needless death and destruction.

---

[52] Ibid.

Jus in bello also requires the fair treatment of prisoners of war. Torture or other forms of mistreatment of these individuals is strictly prohibited. Finally, the principle of *Malum in se* (No Means) disallows the use of inherently "evil" weapons, such as mass rape; forcing enemy combatants to fight against their own flag; or deploying nuclear, biological, or chemical weapons.

The question arises as to whether U.S. troops violated these moral principles during Operation Speedy Express, and throughout the Vietnam War in general, and regrettably, abundant evidence points to the tragic loss of civilian life resulting from Speedy Express. The fundamental principle of Distinction, which directs acts of war toward enemy combatants, makes clear that civilian villagers should not have been targeted. However, for American servicemen, distinguishing between Viet Cong, their sympathizers, and innocent civilians wearing "black pajamas" was an impossible task. This principle requires opposing forces to wear uniforms, for the protection of the civilian population. [53]

---

[53] Tomi Pfanner, Editor-in-Chief, International Review of the Red Cross. "Military Uniforms and the

Conversely, the principle of Distinction held little weight from the perspective of the Viet Cong or the PAVN. In their view, all Americans were legitimate targets, as their presence in Vietnam was synonymous with prosecuting a war, irrespective of their military or civilian roles. Determining whether the principle of Proportionality was violated by U.S. troops proves challenging. Entire hamlets and villages were occasionally destroyed based on suspicions, sometimes accurate, of enemy presence and supply networks. This ambiguity also applies to the principle of Military Necessity.

Compounding the ethical complexities, evidence suggests that both the Viet Cong and the PAVN engaged in numerous acts of terror: attacking, assassinating, and causing harm to civilians and their property, most visibly during the Tet Offensive.

Moreover, the principle of Fair Treatment of Prisoners of War, prohibiting torturing, killing, or otherwise mistreating POWs, was not universally upheld. There is substantial evidence supporting the

---

Law of War." International Committee of the Red Cross. 31-03-2004, Article # 853..

fact that such acts against those who no longer posed a threat were perpetrated by all sides during the conflict.

While the U.S. did not employ nuclear, biological, or chemical weapons (excluding defoliants like Agent Orange, which fall outside this category), they did utilize napalm and overwhelming firepower against an enemy heavily reliant on small arms. Incidences of rape have also been documented.

The Viet Cong, on their part, employed a range of tactics against American soldiers, including the use of poison-laced pungi sticks and various types of booby traps. Additionally, they resorted to acts of terror that targeted their own people, as mentioned earlier.

Drawing conclusions about whether a combatant adhered to the limits prescribed by the Just War Theory is a challenging task. Indeed, it is likely that strict adherence to such principles is impossible within the context of war. Nonetheless, it is worth contemplating the fact that American soldiers, in numerous instances, failed to demonstrate behaviors that align with the values that the nation has long espoused.

  Somewhat fittingly, Operation Speedy Express and debates over it began almost around the time the My Lai Massacre came to light. As the horrific details of that massacre began to leak out, a powerful sense of shock and disgust ran through sections of the American public. In December 1969, the journalist Jonathan Schell, writing in the *New Yorker*, commented, "When others committed them, we looked on the atrocities through the eyes of the victims. Now we find ourselves, almost against our will, looking through the eyes of the perpetrators." Like many others, Schell, who had actually reported from Quang Ngai province around the time of the massacre, felt that the horror of My Lai spoke to deeper truths about the American war effort in Vietnam: "There can be no doubt that such an atrocity was possible only because a number of other methods of killing civilians and destroying their villages had come to be the rule, and not the exception, in our conduct of the war."

  In a similar vein, Senator George McGovern, already a firm opponent of the war, opined that "what this incident has done is tear the mask off the war." In waging war in Vietnam, the United States had "stumbled into a conflict where we not only of necessity commit horrible atrocities against the people of Vietnam, but where in a sense we brutalize our own people and our own nation…I think a national policy is on trial."

McGovern

Supporters of the war effort, while often horrified and outraged at the atrocities, were more likely to see them as a glaring exception and the tragic actions of a few misguided criminals, not an illustration of the true nature of the conflict. For example, Army Secretary Stanley Rogers Resor advised the press, "What occurred at My Lai is wholly unrepresentative of the manner in which our forces conduct military operations in Vietnam…Our men operate under detailed directives which prohibit in unambiguous terms the killing of civilian noncombatants under circumstances such as those of My Lai."

Official contradictions aside, tracing the trajectory of U.S. military involvement in Vietnam reveals a significant shift in the nature of the battles. Initially, large-scale confrontations between substantial armies took place in remote areas, far from densely populated regions. However, as the war dragged on, combat increasingly shifted to urban settings or areas near population centers, inevitably exposing civilians to the perils of warfare. In particular, 1968 marked a turning point, and the unwavering resolve of the United States to continue fighting began to crumble. This was a period when an inquisitive press and a growing sense of disillusionment among the troops brought to light an increasing number of accounts detailing atrocities and the targeting of noncombatants by both sides. These stories were plastered across television screens, newspapers, and magazines worldwide, leaving a profound impact.

There is no more significant instance of this sea change in public opinion than the very public agony of *CBS* newsman Walter Cronkite. Cronkite's conversion from supporter to outspoken war skeptic, simultaneously a cause, an effect, and a microcosm of the larger national reassessment, did not come easily. While his doubts about the war effort had multiplied in the years preceding Tet, he had been hesitant to abandon his public stance as an objective journalist:

> "I had resisted doing commentary on the *Evening News* even when it had been suggested to me. I was concerned about whether it's possible as a professional journalist to wear two hats. But when Tet came along, the public was already divided

and confused. We had been told that the war was practically over, that there was light at the end of the tunnel, that we had won the hearts and minds, that the Viet Cong was decreasing in strength and popular support, and then suddenly it can conduct a military operation of the scale and the intensity that it did in Tet. Well, everybody was throwing up their hands saying "God, what in the world is happening out there?" And we decided that we had pretty good credibility of having been as impartial as it's possible to be, and maybe it's time to go out there and just do some pieces on what it looks like and try to give some guidance.

"My personal approach had been impartial because I found it hard to make up my own mind. In the early stages I thought we should be involved in trying to preserve a territory where democracy might be permitted to flourish in Southeast Asia. I began to get opposed when the military commitment was made. I didn't think we ought to have our troops there. And then I got more and more concerned as more and more troops [went out]. My particular concern was that the Administration did not tell us the truth about the nature or size of the commitment that was going to be required. And I think that's where the Administration lost the support of the American people—in trying to pretend it was something we could do with our left hand, without asking the people at home to share the heavy responsibility. At any rate, I went out there and what I saw led me to the conclusions that I made."

Describing South Vietnam as a "burned and blasted and weary land," Cronkite announced, "We have been too often disappointed by the optimism of the American leaders. . . . To say that we are closer to victory today is to believe, in the face of evidence, the optimists who have been wrong in the past…To say that we are mired in stalemate seems the only realistic, yet unsatisfactory conclusion…It seems now more certain than ever that the bloody experience of Vietnam is to end in a stalemate…It is increasingly clear to this reporter that the only rational way out then will be to negotiate, not as victors, but as honorable people who lived up to their pledge to defend democracy, and did the best they could."

President Johnson allegedly responded to Cronkite's report with the comment, "If I've lost Cronkite, I've lost middle America." Reflecting on events much later, Cronkite himself was surprised by the impact of his commentary, and particularly its effect on the president: "I didn't expect it to be that effective It should have shocked the President only if he didn't know the full scale of the thing himself. I think he may have been as surprised by Tet as everybody else was, and while the military was putting up a brave front 'Oh, boy, we sucked them right into our trap and we've given them a great, magnificent military blow from which they'll never recover'—it was an optimism that, my God, you couldn't see on the ground out there. The Viet Cong was right in the city of Saigon. That was what kind of turned so many of us at that point into saying, 'Come on, now. This is the end. Stop it.'" (Willenson, 196).

Cronkite in Vietnam

In such a poisonous, confused atmosphere, official claims of an American victory, whatever their merits, were bound to ring hollow. As Vermont Senator George Aiken declared, "If this is a failure, I hope the Viet Cong never have a major success."

Online Resources

Other books about Vietnam by Charles River Editors

Further Reading

Dale Andrade, James H. Willbanks. "CORDS/Phoenix – Counterinsurgency Lessons from Vietnam for the Future." Military Review. March/April 2006.

Trent Angers. The Forgotten Hero of My Lai: The Hugh Thompson Story. Lafayette, LA, Acadian House.

Kevin Buckley. "Pacification's Deadly Price." Newsweek. 19 June 1972.

Marcus Tullius Cicero, Walter Miller. De Officiis. With an English translation by Walter Miller. Robarts – University of Toronto. 1913.

Edward Doyle, Samuel Lipsman, Terrence Maitland. The Vietnam Experience. Boston Publishing Company, 1978.

Edward Doyle, Samuel Lipsman, Stephen Weiss. Passing the Torch. Boston, MA. 1981.

Lyndon B. Johnson. Speeches: "Remarks on Decision to Not Seek Re-Election." March 31, 1966. Miller Center of Public Affairs, Scripps Library &

Multimedia Archive. The University of Virginia.

R.K. Bringham. Guerilla Diplomacy: The NLFs Foreign Relations and the Vietnam War.

Adam Jones. Genocide: A Comprehensive Introduction. Taylor and Francis, 2010.

Howard Jones. My Lai: Vietnam 1968 and the Descent into Darkness. Oxford University Press, 2017.

D. Coleman. Choppers: The Heroic Birth of Helicopter Warfare. New York. St. Martin's Press, 1988.

Rosemary Giles, Guest Author. "The Controversial Phoenix Program Was Created to Obliterate the Viet Cong" War History Online May 17, 2023.

Charles Guthrie, Michael Quinlan. The Just War: Ethics in Modern Warfare. Walker Books, London.

Interview with Col. David Hackworth, USA, South Vietnam. "Guerilla Wars." People's Century, PBS.

Guenter Levy. America in Vietnam. Oxford University Press, New York. 1978.

Michael Lanning, Dan Cragg. <u>Inside the VC and the NVA</u>. Ballantine Books. 1993

Samuel Lipsman, Edward Doyle. <u>The Vietnam Experience: Fighting for Time</u>. Boston: Boston Publishing Company, 1983. pp. 50-54.

John Morocco. <u>The Vietnam Experience: Thunder From Above: Air War 1941-1968.</u> Boston Publishing Company, 1968.

Mark Moyar. <u>Phoenix and the Birds of Prey: The CIA's Secret Campaign to Destroy the Viet Cong</u>. United States Naval Institute Press. 2007.

Douglas Pike. <u>The Vietcong Strategy of Terror</u>. PDF. U.S. Mission, Saigon. February 1970.

Donald Porter "Cobras and Loaches, two vastly different aircraft, relied on each other to fight the enemy. In Vietnam, These Helicopter Scouts Saw Combat Up Close." <u>Air & Space Magazine</u>. September 2017.

Tomi Pfanner, Editor-in-Chief, <u>International Review of the Red Cross</u>. "Military Uniforms and the Law of War." International Committee of the

Red Cross. 31-03-2004, Article # 853.

Ami Predhazhur. Root Causes of Suicide Terrorism: The Globalization of Martyrdom. Taylor & Francis. 2006

Thomas W. Scoville. Reorganizing for Pacification Support. Archived 06-29-2019, Wayback Machine, Center of Military History, U.S. Army, 1982.

John Sherwood. "Defending the Mekong Delta: Tet and the Legacy of the Brown Water Navy." War on the Rocks. January 31, 2018.

Capt. Jack Shulimson. U.S. Marines in Vietnam: The Defining Year 1968. (Marine Corps Series).

Heather Stur. "The Viet Cong Committed Atrocities Too." The New York Times. December 19, 2017.

Scott W. Thompson, Donaldson D. Frizzel. The Lessons of Vietnam. New York, Crane, Russak & Co. 1977.

Nick Turse. Kill Anything That Moves: The Real American War in Vietnam. Metropolitan Books. 2013

Michael Walzer. Just and Unjust Wars : A Moral Argument with Historical Illustrations. New York, Basic Books, 1977.

Geoffrey C. Ward and Ken Burns. The Vietnam War – An Intimate History. Introduction by Ken Burns and Lynn Novick. Alfred A. Knopf, New York, 2017. p. XII.

"Phoenix Program in the Vietnam War." Facts and Details. May 2014.

"Counterinsurgency in Vietnam: Lessons for Today." The Foreign Service Journal. April 2015.

Peers Report (Report of the Investigation of the My Lai Massacre) by General R. Peers. "My Lai Courts Marital Page: The Omission and Commission of Capt. Ernest L. Medina."

"U.S. Involvement in the Vietnam War: The Tet Offensive 1969." Department of the Historian, Bureau of Public Affairs, U.S. Department of State. December 28, 2018.

Made in the USA
Columbia, SC
30 August 2023

ac609b58-a02e-4535-b95c-89ece863f87cR01